Yes, You Can, Moses!

illustrated by
ANDY STILES
based on the book by Sandy Brooks

The Standard Publishing Company, Cincinnati, Ohio. A division of Standex International Corporation.
© 1996 by The Standard Publishing Company. Printed in the United States of America.
All rights reserved. Designed by Coleen Davis. ISBN 0-7847-0434-1.

God talked to Moses from a burning bush. "Bring my people out of Egypt!" God said. "I can't," said Moses.

"Yes, you can, Moses," said God.

Then Moses and his brother Aaron
went to Egypt to see the king.
But the king wouldn't let God's people go.

So God sent trouble to Egypt . . .

Finally the king let God's people go free.

But when they were gone,
the king changed his mind.
He sent his army after God's people.

So God sent a strong wind to part the sea,
and the people walked across on dry ground.

The king's army tried to follow
God's people into the sea.

But God let go of the water,
and God's people were safe.

"There's no one like you, God,"
said Moses.
"And now I know I can do
anything you ask,
if I just follow you
and do what you say."